The *Victory Garden*
VEGETABLE
Alphabet Book

by Jerry Pallotta
and Bob Thomson

Illustrated by
Edgar Stewart

Charlesbridge

For Aunt Cindy McEachern and her great garden. — J.P.
To my grandchildren Todd and Brad. — B.T.
To Annie and Katie with love. — E.S.

Copyright © 1992
by Jerry Pallotta.
Illustrations Copyright © 1992
by Edgar Stewart.

Published by
Charlesbridge Publishing
85 Main Street
Watertown, MA 02172
(617) 926-0329

Library of Congress
Catalog Card Number 92-71580
ISBN 0-88106-468-8 (softcover)
ISBN 0-88106-469-6 (hardcover)
ISBN 0-88106-685-0 (library reinforced)

Printed in the United States of America
(sc) 10 9 8 7 6 5 4 3
(hc) 10 9 8 7 6 5 4 3 2

Books by Jerry Pallotta:
The Icky Bug Alphabet Book
The Bird Alphabet Book
The Ocean Alphabet Book
The Flower Alphabet Book
The Yucky Reptile Alphabet Book
The Frog Alphabet Book
The Furry Alphabet Book
The Dinosaur Alphabet Book
The Underwater Alphabet Book
The Victory Garden Vegetable Alphabet Book
The Extinct Alphabet Book
The Desert Alphabet Book
The Make Your Own Alphabet Book
Going Lobstering
The Icky Bug Counting Book
Cuenta los insectos

Bob Thomson is the former host of The Victory Garden®
on public television. The TV series and other Victory
Garden books are produced by WGBH-Boston.

Special thanks to: Julia, Matthew, Marie, Johnny,
Patrick, Elizabeth, Todd, Brad, Chester, Andrew, Tara,
Katie, Patrick, Heather, Adam, Sara, Jillian, Essence,
Takorian, Spencer, Kimberly and Matt.

When planting a garden, the first thing we have to do is prepare the soil. The ground needs to be turned over. Any sticks and stones should be tossed aside. We then might add compost to enrich the soil. Ultimately, we want the soil to be loose and level.

Oops! Here is a vegetable ready to harvest.

A is for Asparagus. We do not have to plant the Asparagus because it is a perennial. It stays in the ground and sprouts new shoots every year.

Aa

Now it is time to plant the seeds in our garden. The seeds should be spaced properly and planted according to the directions on the seed packets.

Nature will work its magic and soon the seeds will grow into beautiful vegetables.

Bb

B is for Beet. This is a root vegetable. The Beet greens that grow above the ground can also be eaten. Some people like the Beet greens better than the Beets.

Worms and toads are good for your garden. Hey, worm, wiggle your way to the W page where you belong!

Cc

C is for Carrot. Carrots are one of the few vegetables that are bright orange in color. Of course, people are not the only ones who love Carrots!

D is for Daikon. Daikon is a white radish that is shaped like a big, fat carrot. In this book, the letter D should be for Difficult page. We had a hard time finding a vegetable that begins with the letter D.

Dd

E is for Eggplant.
Years ago, Eggplants were deep purple. Now, gardeners can grow bright white Eggplants. Some are called Ghostbusters and others are called Caspers.

Ee

F is for Fiddleheads. Fiddleheads are young ferns that are harvested before they uncurl. If you want Fiddleheads in your garden, though, they would have to be transplanted from the wild.

Ff

G is for Greenbean. Greenbeans have great nutritional value. That is why your parents make you eat them! A fun way to grow Greenbeans is to let the bean vines climb up the legs of a teepee.

Gg

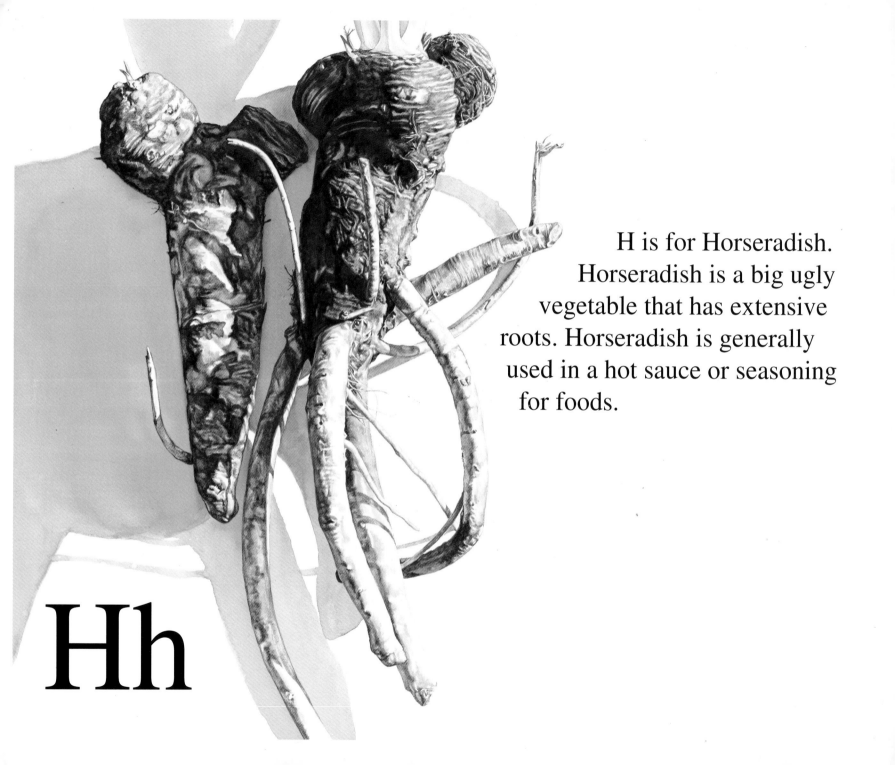

H is for Horseradish. Horseradish is a big ugly vegetable that has extensive roots. Horseradish is generally used in a hot sauce or seasoning for foods.

Hh

I is for Indian Corn. This corn has hard colorful kernels. Indian Corn is primarily used for ornamental purposes, especially around Thanksgiving. People do not usually eat it.

Indian Corn For Sale

Ii

J is for Jalapeño. You are in for a big surprise if you bite into a Jalapeño Pepper. This is a hot, hot, hot vegetable. Eating one will make your mouth and throat feel like they are on fire. Jalapeños can even make you cry.
Be careful.

Jj

K is for Kohlrabi. Kohlrabi is more common in Europe than in North America. The many thick stems of this vegetable make it look like an alien spaceship with lots of antennas.

Kk

L is for Leek. Leeks are easy to grow and are naturally pest free. Insects and animals do not like to eat them. Leeks can be harvested early when they are as small as your baby finger, or later in the year when they are as long as your arm.

Ll

Mm

M is for Munchkin.
Munchkins are little
tiny pumpkins
that can fit in
the palm of
your hand. Giant
mammoth pumpkins
grow so large that
you have to call
someone with a
forklift or a
backhoe to pick
them up.

N is for Norland Potato.
Potatoes grow underground. There are almost three hundred different types of potatoes worldwide. Not all potatoes have brown or yellow skin. There are even red, white, or blue potatoes. The Norland Potato has red skin.

Nn

O is for Okra. When picking Okra, you have to be extra careful you do not pull down the whole stalk. Okra is an excellent soup thickener. Okra is also called Gumbo.

Oo

Pp

P is for Peanut. Peanuts have an unusual way of growing. As the stems of the Peanut plant grow upward, some shoots turn downward and bury themselves. The peanuts actually grow underground.

If we are going to have some peanuts in this book, we might as well have some popcorn.

P is
also for Popcorn.
Popcorn kernels
are smaller than
sweet corn that
people eat. When
Popcorn kernels are
dried, they still hold
some moisture. If they
are heated up, the
moisture expands
and pop, pop, pop
goes the Popcorn.

Q is for Quicksilver. Most corn is yellow, but Quicksilver is the nickname of a silvery white sweet corn. It is fun to play hide-and-go-seek in the corn stalks.

Qq

R is for Radicchio.
Radicchio is an Italian vegetable
like lettuce, but it is not green. Fancy restaurants
often use Radicchio as a decoration because of its unique
color. The people who eat Radicchio enjoy its slightly bitter taste.

S is for Snowpeas. Snowpeas grow well in the cool spring weather. Sometimes you may even see the rows of peas covered in snow. This is how they got their name. Snowpeas seem perfectly happy after a snowstorm.

Ss

Tt

T is for Turnip.
Turnips are one of the
fastest growing root crops.
One kind of big Turnip
is called a Rutabaga.
Rutabaga is a funny name.

Uu

U is for Ultra Girl.
Ultra Girl is the   name of a
really beautiful tomato. Boys should not
be mad though. There is also a little
larger tomato that is called Ultra
Boy. Tomatoes are the most
common vegetables grown in gardens.

V is for Victory Cucumber. Did you know that pickles are cucumbers? Remember, keep your hand out of the pickle jar.

V is also for Victory Garden. Victory Garden is the name given to gardens that families grew to help feed people during World War II. While farm-grown vegetables were being shipped overseas to the troops, families were encouraged to grow their own "Victory Gardens."

Vv

W is for Walla Walla. There are at least three special sweet onions. There is the Walla Walla from the Pacific Northwest, the Vidalia from Georgia, and the Maui from Hawaii. But even a sweet onion can bring tears to your eyes.

Ww

Xx

X is for Xeriscaping. Xeriscaping is the art
of growing plants with hardly any water.
This is a new word and a whole new type
of outdoor landscaping and gardening
that preserves our precious water.

Y is for Yard Long Bean. This bean can grow to be about 36 inches long. You can use it for a belt, you can pretend it is a jumprope, or you can cook it and have a very long lunch.

Woodchuck, you should go to the W page, too.

Yy

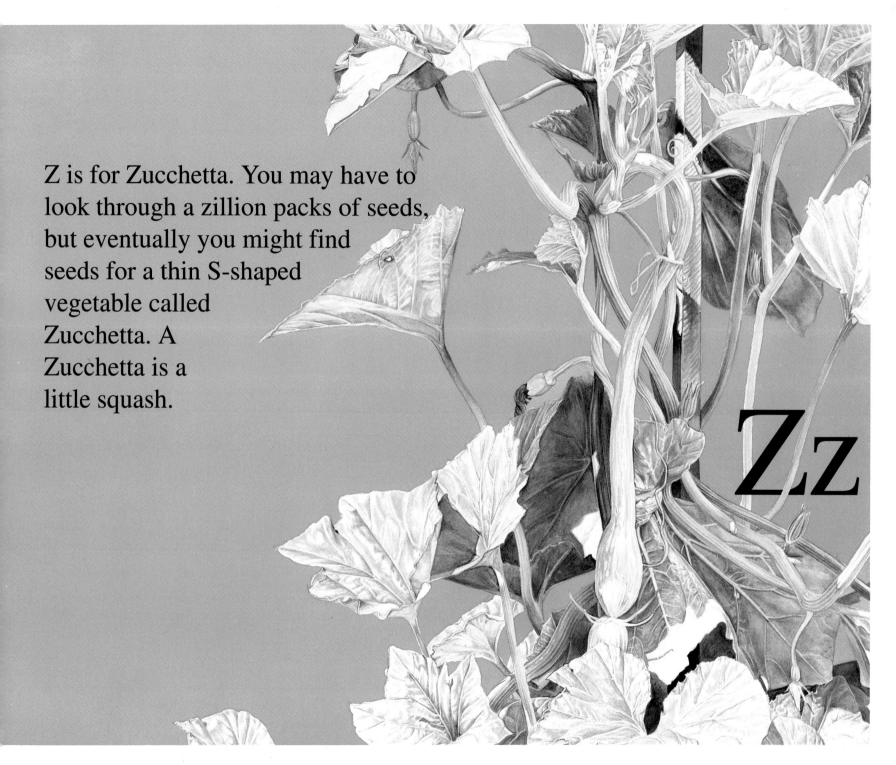

Z is for Zucchetta. You may have to look through a zillion packs of seeds, but eventually you might find seeds for a thin S-shaped vegetable called Zucchetta. A Zucchetta is a little squash.

Zz

Winter is coming and now it is time to put the Victory Garden to bed.
Good night Victory Garden.

The End